The Reaches

Ansgar Allen

First published in 2021 by

Schism Nεuronics

First edition

ISBN: 9798571561907

To accompany *Ice* by Emile Bojesen, released by Geräuschmanufaktur in 2021
https://geraeuschmanufaktur.bandcamp.com/

Written
to accompany
Emile Bojesen's *Ice*

composed
to accompany
The Reaches

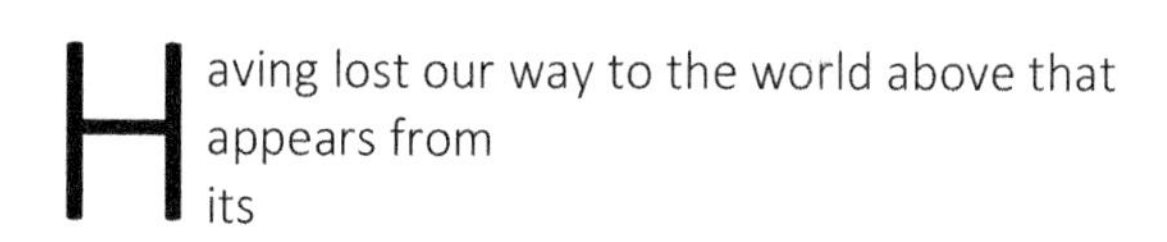

aving lost our way to the world above that
appears from
its

other appeal
broken
and
torn to the reaches

none talked

shards
limits
against ice
or

the memory of desert sand resting against the city we
abandoned

fallen
then, toward the
edges of which I
spat

they spat
we spat together
and the moisture rolled itself in a ball

coated by dust

exiles

by that point

silenced
sentenced
sentences waiting.

The ice shelf groans above us
now, limbs raised, floated

pit your ears against it
flotation
devices, though

not the tongue
which sticks to
structures from a time that moved
extending toward the vision board, past centre, of what
the earth
our moon

frozen still, the water

surfaces, and creatures passing

by

dead

or hardly living

unknown

to those who enter these depths with
different intent

the globular structure broken now prodded
distending waves
tearing edge
centuries old, the torch
inside
to
watch it glow

these others

they travelled

unheeded

moved

by killing, or breaking, but were

never here nobody

has

been exactly

here

there

where architecture is its worst and cannot be

described

and we find ourselves abutting

ice

the parts protrude

as we travel, or hardly drift, bellies up   the sunlight
that makes its way
even where
the ice is thickest   and the mountain

to the horizon
at the edges of the sea

and the shore at the base of it
some kind of dwelling

a ruin

visited
last
before we were born and began to retreat.

Stuff of my mouth preoccupied me
as I drifted, unsaid

there is no speaking here, it occupied us all who
spat once in the desert and turned, I spat, they spat, we
spat together, where indeed, who has done under those
conditions will not know the spectacle, dust rolled up
spherical, refusing to flatten its
film

taken from the path since landing
five degrees to the left, ten to the right, north

south

the outer suburbs inundated, the centre empty and

cracked

a magnet held the needle as the current took each part
to a part of the shelf where none would choose to live

stranded awhile
belly up
still, caught between

one formation
and
the other

looking across feet, there are too many feet, too many footprints on the

moon   already, no spit, no humans except those who threaten to come
and us, what we are, laid out and compelled by hatred, or at least knowledge

afterthoughts

no weed down here   hardly any light.

Crustaceans avoid us

we made attempts, what, say it then, and judged each piece badly
else

knowing it only by the rim, agitators once

falsely

taken by the cacophony we created
no

that the mountain threw back from its edifice and the
globular structure absorbed indifferent, silenced sentenced

each magma chamber empty
the last meal turned out.

Before we took to the sea   its crust, when
economies would suffer   before the invention
a device that froze all ideals and

bodies of   lives lived by them

diminishing our liberty
closing down our economy is worse

they said

in the face of it fungal treatments applied to their toes
what you fear

say it then, they said

trading death against what, and then then

I understand that

what

these lives are vitally important but

they added

which was when we killed them
or allowed them to

kill themselves

telling as they died
our naivety
when

about how business works

their grimaces set
minds unthinking
each death mask already in place.

W as
before
we took
to the edges

having heard them say

this
is what business
is trained to do

and

weren't we deficient in our thinking

and doing too

as we talked
of death economies

and

the death of their word, and

the death in their words

as they told us that the best that can be done is to mitigate
the death situation, the death situation, they said to us

and we looked back and threw the switch and saw them
die by the devices they constructed

their death situation, our death situation not yet, but the
pulse has thickened

the ice was still forming at the edges of the sea, there were
gaps
closing but wide enough
to enter, the world above sealed off from itself

a crust to walk on where those who tell themselves
we humans finally halted and looked

to their feet.

We below have begun to wonder what bellies are
or what bellies represented
when appetites or something, hunger
possessed innards

each cavern made its demands   they say, each chamber
possessed its idol

the walls

were
        lined

with milk   not milk, they said, but these walls

were
bleached

by
radiating light that falsified the surface and
rendered it flat.

The idols were disposed of by their own radiation and
the return of microbes too

amoeboid life
from the gaps that connected one
chamber to another, enlargements
or
cracks

that had not been
noticed until that point an argument
against
their

independence and the religious orders
technological ones

too, of caverns, and crevices

that spread and
suffused with decay

called belief

passed across catacombs and
other networks   and the buildings
                                              now razed

that once produced their
own   subterranean world
above ground for the life of
idols, gathered up

dropped from between clouds of

sulphur, called bombs

to pit the earth too flat to live on, depressions are

needed

even if the wet runs in
and pools
at the base

as places to study, and think, or do what thinking was once called, charts arranged against the sides of each crater with formulas that described the surrounding wastelands

other craters, and the art of fenestration

the purpose of which was known to none other than the

eye which peered at each window
and spectated each crater

industrious beings turning themselves over, sliding
imperceptibly, to the lowest part where the wet
accumulated and mingled

the lowest part is worse than the highest part
but not as good as the middle part, they suggested, by
moving a little each   every part that slid to maintain
position where the charts were handled, tools incorporated
at the base, for puckering the earth

or sides, in smaller pits that served as grips and purchases

these ones that called themselves humans
and looked from one crater to the next, puckered gaze
cracked lips, dust crossing the rim and descending
to the wet, before the wet dried up and the sun beat down
and the charts were raised for shade, the formulas
forgotten, all fenestration declaimed as hostile
to the labour of life in a crater
which is better than life on the flat, now walls are gone
and bricks are dust, and the dust congeals
and materials no longer yield to their intentions.

Life on the flat has no idols
or places of retreat, and fancy

or succour

or hidden

violence.

Before the bombs were lifted, and dropped, they sat
with sticks to beat the ground, the dust of which
rose, and gathered, the mouth open

it was known as the eat.

The dust, turned liquid
cooled solid

as particulates forced themselves and their impulses
to amalgamate

this was known as the flattening

where

the eat was against the flattening
and the flattening produced the eat.

Beaches turned   to glass, and the pounding
started   once more for the eat, and the eat
recommenced the sitting as tides passed over

surfaces

where the weed no longer caught, or the crabs had
foothold, and spaces

they called them forerunners

found no means of marking time   cogs turned blunt
against the softer parts   turned hard

their electrolytes settling

halting

at their destinations in any case   if not actually ceasing
to exist, and the electrons refusing to communicate sound
or sense, to those instruments that were held to determine
the cause

and they heard by other means.

Some came face to face again, with others
their faces, they were overcome with
emotion described as massive, although flies
landed and pulled that out due suction

the limbs of flies are pneumatic chambers and their
protruding mouths drained, these others responded
the flies were indifferent to that, but that
it seemed
was sufficient occasion from which some found solace
even if others knew that the eggs could not hatch because
the meat was hormone rich, and the hormones were
misdirected, or misinterpreted by organisms
that had no use for stimuli

or prompts, what managers call invitations

although invitations are orders

and orders are a form of malice

an invitation to destroy

any being

that has not receded to its hollow

or

given in to stupefaction

linguistic forms

would you like to
    may I suggest
    could I venture, and so on

that manufacture pleasantries   still

just as they produce sycophants

these creatures with legs
and hands that stick, working

as an extension of organs that inflate and burrow, each
limb pushed straight by pressure

which is why spiders die in balls

the pressure having dropped.

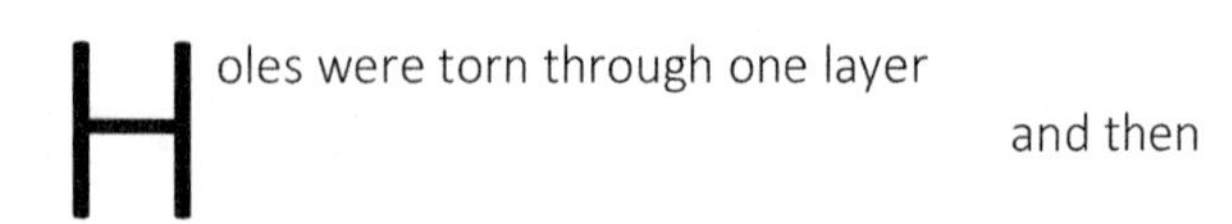

Holes were torn through one layer

and then

from the one met next to the next after that

laminae broken and pierced

once more

by the organs that inflated

and then burrowed, or burrowed as they inflated, and
injected their venom

as diaries were consulted, and filled, as the lines started
and the lines stopped

the surveys were sent and retracted
and the purpose of intention was lost

this moment

which was known as the sit.

One

feature

of that world

the one that came to sit

its greater evils so pronounced none would see
them, if seeing them meant feeling them
when feeling them meant being their

target

if only at the level of perception, initially
sufficient that

and the margins of perception   the lesser evils
diminished by contrast, yet far more numerous
were forgotten too, or never readily   perceived

which is how destruction happened

with the sycophants

and servants of industry

in the van, advancing with the rest somehow, held, if not
at one time struggling

raked from their moorings, trailing their   chains and
reluctant themselves to see their injuries, or their extent

because vision clouds before excess

or pain

and futility

which made others laugh

and garrot themselves with it

but laughter cannot be understood, and so they were
diminished in turn and ceased eventually to laugh.

Pitched in place and less
then still, the vats, already known and sawn in half
for dwelling places, as said

before, once, before

the wind took them to the

other place, the other place

they said

doors thrown open by outsiders who chanted its name

the real name

of the

other place

that those in the chamber would not

utter

for reasons that function as traditions, and traditions that serve, again, to dull reason
and would usually suffice

to keep nothing from happening, in the context
of so much noise, being taught, from a very young age, that
the stasis which is should be celebrated
each year following, to allow the years be counted
to follow each other stacked, and revered, and
heavy with inertia.

That was when walls still stood, and bricks
held their form coffins too, taking less
when less was more than before

appetites grew beyond the capacity to digest, and
remainders began to accumulate.

All places of rest were studded to prevent recliners

so recliners did   upright and at work

when work was available, or in their own time
when time was referred to that way

still, as a possession

even though it slips from hands to make mischief
between its records, and pauses

those moments when   something, elsewhere
always resumes   a steel girder set in place
perhaps

or a message sent

and the scream, a mantis

places itself   across the inner ear

and declares there be no silence.

Even after the eat
the sit
the flattening, the silence did not come

below the ice there is still sound
including tectonic movement
the magma convects

if not because the core is frozen due to residual heat
the core has sent out its last wave become solid

must halt rotation, shall turn one face to the sun

and the other

to the stars

and will render there be no difference between crust and
the planetary innards.

Ours may be the light side

or the dark side

it is not yet determined.

As a footnote to the culture that grew, and changed and was lost to itself

philosophy met its end in words that unfurled and laughed at wisdom, emitting sounds that interrupted reason-making and the possession of selves in arguments of which arguments never constituted selves, but were once believed to

the belief itself dying, another joke

or showing itself up

that death, if not of philosophy, but certainly of the philosopher, being foretold and persistently forgotten

they forgot it
and held themselves philosophers still
words pronounced with   meaning

               sentences bound together as grandiose gestures
to the strength of mind and the force of its gesture

                              so we annihilated them too, the ones
                               who called themselves philosophers

or watched them annihilate themselves

speaking

clarifying

arguing against their irrelevance
never facing that
to do so entailed the holding of heads in stomachs
or against the groin

so

we held their heads for them and watched them

begin to speak

as they finally learned to utter words from mouths that no longer lingered on the words produced but projected them outwards as fast as the words foretold themselves from crevices and recesses in the cheek

and the neck, the darker regions of the face

where they returned once said and spoke of the void

dysfluent

tirelessly   repeating

some words extended across hours that connected one night to another

          declaring its presence

inexhaustibly verbose and worse than silence, switching register, refusing to settle out there was no sediment to their speech

we saw it when   it did not settle, where indeed, this
we, when we said it, referred to a future we, not yet
realised, and so

we

did not speak on behalf of a group, because
this we does not exist, nor do
we
as we float   exist together

surely nothing unites us

but the abjection that causes us to settle against the ice
as a them over there, then, that declares no community
and has no sun   our we refers to a future that we
have   vanquished, as an idea, as they declared it

we who sat on each other's pieces and continued until
there were none left to eviscerate, even those that fell
under desks and found their way to the cash register, and
circulated

until they were entirely run down, could not hold
themselves to a declaration

a shared experience that united them
or made them similar enough
or sympathetic enough to one another

to throw chains into their wheels

so to halt, or fall, in a configuration

of bodies that seemed
for that moment
related.

Ice does not halt when it reaches the body and decide
this growth has met its limit

which is how bodies came to moor under the shelf
and were incorporated, unless disturbed

in which case they broke off again with appendages.

Bodies with appendages drift differently from bodies without

hesitantly, struck to rotate

hit then turning

wrenched at base

extended beyond the belly

and organs grown branches of themselves

hearts adopting the same crystalline structure that

then

interpenetrates

fed outward by the inward freeze

just as the outward freeze fed inward

facets each

generating growth across the chambers

with none to see them
and dissect the innards
and declare them this or that

the earth
the slab

suffered worse

hidden recesses in crust, caves filled with water
against inspection to drown those who went too far

    but those who went brought machinery, and, to the greatest caves, uncurled their pipes and pumped all water out, the chamber filled with gas, still bad to breathing

the spaces

light goes more easily

less bent   through air

photography has greater reach   and footprints

tear structure downward, not upward

this reveal, the structures

it allowed them be lit, walked upon

and imaged before the liquid returned from the base

the geode

filled

around the columns, each crystal, as the divers departed
and halted the engines that stole the earth its dark

or

what some called liquid density.

Though the earth stole it back just as surely
and later froze it over

the gaps closing further north as we came from the mountain

by the way of the ruin

to enter the reaches these parts

where space to fall, still fell, to the place below

between ice
and rock, the sea, regions

to the edge of which the liquid space thins out in the
direction of shore

some become pinned there

between ice and rock

with structures

grown inward

just as they grow outward, meeting

and then laterally to form a trunk
that binds the shelf to the floor

more surely through the body, we think, than without.

The mountain and the ruin somehow not been met by
the flattening that did level all other, and elsewhere

and produced the eat
to assuage the flattening
that turned sand to glass
and soil to glaze

not much left beyond that, then, to ingest, except the dust
that was the eat, it not being recorded

if the eat preceded the flattening

or

if the flattening gave rise to the eat

but the eat did happen after
pound the earth, it said

when the earth was flat as that
and no bit held up the view
but the people who did kneel, or sit

and perform the eat.

Dust earth give up did block the throat but stuck like solid

some fell down and fill the stomach

the feel of which was stone.

The things they dropped, they called it bombing, did
make dust too that fill the oesophagus
as the trunk was known

living fossils, they said, the pounding by the bomb
replaced the pounding by the sticks

till the dust settled and fell to glass.

Glass could not be eat.

Craters made the flat
that was the earth
have some relief, the water too did pool

whereas on the flat it did not

rendered upward from the base, droplets do not spread
they run to one another repelled by the flat

each drop turns in at the fall the edge

to leave the earth prematurely

drops rising to spheres, not steam

become orbs

they hit these orbs with sticks, only then did orbs be steam
and cloud the bit above the rising.

Some would never be cloud
or be rising so would
join the sit.

After the eat the body with the stone inside does
begin to transit
become dust and the dust be glass, hence

structure in human form, they called it human, falls to flat
also, eventually as a consequence of the eat.

The flat is human stone be glass, in part
the stomach
the mouth
the gut, the circumference of the earth

with the gut stone a finer glass, the dust has passage
and the water sits on what regardless

human stone glass
mountain stone glass
city stone glass, and curves, then ascends from the flat
most of it not hit by those who, pausing from the eat
struck up, not down.

Flat was not created in a day
each city breathed out its idols as surface caves
rooms, halls, cellars, lost walls to dust, bondage gone
vapour rising too

that left those who moved about each city
a different prospect with no places to dwell
or corners to shelter

nor idols to house and seal off from other idols

they crawled with their idols
from one open cavern to another

as the walls caved in, no place to hide them

but in crawling knew, the idols must not meet
or the need of them be seen
and the friction between them happen

it might state itself and determine against the holding of
idols, but the idols met and this meeting deranged belief

they crawled still after, but differently now
having no idols to hold, so they lived in their absence

somehow

no holes to put them in to visit
to abandon, to imprison their hope

which is, after all, how hope be sustained, in blueprints, or
affects, chained to idols, as idol blueprints, idol affects
prison vistas

but the idols gone
and chambers have corners

the corners fell, even the thickest walls lasting longest

having corners, buttresses, reinforced parts

all concrete that had steels burst
most concrete then, reinforced

metal sublimates whereas rock disintegrates and then coagulates

so the flat is rock come together
and the sky is steel, an alloy

of something and something else.

The sky being filled with idol, risen

a foul stench, as well as alloy cloud

did cause them turn to see it

the spectacle was tar and blindness, oil most probably too
the colour of it refusing to divide, but hardly whiteness
either

        wavelengths overlaid to something those who
determined sight, called meat, but the meat hypothesis did
not register

so most called it cloud, but to call it cloud, the memory
of cloud, had to go, with the memory of rain
what fell having shards most often that struck the mouth
open, and lacerated tongues.

This was called the drink
        the drink happened due to a memory of rain

                the tongue was lacerated by that memory
which persisted, and mouths still opened to the one called
cloud

        alloy lines of which
                        cut across the lips, the gums

but the drink did follow the eat, and the eat will follow the drink, only, after the thing that fell

what they misunderstood as rain
the flat was covered with it

liquid alloy   not shards

arranging in larger groups, pools, that made
pounding with sticks   wet with metal

and the dust get mixed with it, so the pounding stopped, and the eat did pause, until the alloy left the earth by vapourisation.

Then the eat recommenced, the dust flew, and each mouth opened to ingest stone gut, stone anus

the alimentary canal.

From the perspective of which, the prospect was poor then
with the eat giving way to the formation of stone internally, that became the flat and so the end of the one who ate, or, the other prospect, the drink that tore the tongue.

But the drink did hinder the eat
because the lacerated tongue collected the dust
before the dust was swallowed

the dust in the crevices of the tongue formed latticework of stone called cage

that

if it did not enclose the tongue in its cage

fell off from the mouth to the flat, where it too joined the flat, become glass

so the drink was, then

to some extent against the eat, and

the lacerated tongue

the reason why so many survived longer
than the eat proposed.

Fall of the cities, hills

eventually mountains, to the level of the flat
took longer than a day, so the eat did not become
necessary or urgent

until the flattening was finished

this process thereby extending too the prospects of those
still existing who carried
during the period of the flattening

all manner of

bankrupt notions and decrepit manners
of speech and human intercourse to the very
end of that time when the earth showed some kind of
gradient, or relief

a

punctum to measure distance by and
cultivate the sense that one thing can be distinguished
from the next.

Organics
facing the transition of soil to glaze
roots encased, or where seeds fell spread outward
along the surface to their extent

under those conditions, and dried
sucked inward by retraction, I only buy, some said, though
others, most others, took all they could that still grew

or had once grown been canned

the sea was still rising and falling marking time at its edges
by the reach and the fall of the wet, and there was life in it
that might be drawn from the shell, the lips at the rim
creating the vacuum that took the creature from its
purchases, where most of those who still called themselves
humans, and others that did not
trod back to the reaches
the small things washed about the ankles, the toes, or felt
by the feet beneath the sand where burrowed, and taken
for the ritual ingestion that became the memory
that became the eat
this before the sand become glass, the flat, not finished
but largely accomplished, entailed nothing to look
but the others who had nothing to look at too

so they looked at one another, the nothing to look at was
so they looked at, the others looked at one another, when
not disintegrating following the eat, or precisely when
disintegrating following the eat, it being another
perspective on the flat the unbearable nothing.

The sea before frozen was landscape against the flat
it being not only grazing at the rim, opportunities
to grasp what washed in
but relief from the unbearable flat

the flat was oceanic, the sea was froth, the froth was
something to look at, the talk was something to hear it
being the thing that stood for the event, each talk a minor
event, even though talk was no event but the memory of
the world that manufactured the words that had become
the talk

the talk being all repetition and distortion, insistent phrase
with nothing to insist upon, including memory of talk
before the flattening that was repetition and distortion
then too, but was accompanied by things that happened
alongside and made the talk have portent

though portent was a mistaken perception of the engine
of talk, that was language and inertia and physics, having
laws that talk did not touch but only expressed, as noise
heard back as meaning

leaked sideways

tongue to the roof, in lateral, alveolar fricatives

the tongue set to block, halter, and declare torment
inexpressible, this was the reason for the talk before
torment of the flat, the flat did not produce the talk, but
the talk did get on because of it, in the pause between the
eat, the pounding, and the drink, the standing talk was
different to the wandering talk, the standing talk more
desperate in its grammar, declaiming, the wandering talk
carried by the motion to greater fluency and took some
who talked best, fluent, unhalting, and not distracted by
thought-like interruption

to

the furthest points of the flat and to the remaining
mountain upon which they walked, and talked, and drove
themselves beyond the violence of law

and the organising constraint of language

to wavelengths of speech that, overlaid

did obliterate all remaining sense

this was the point that they

or we or those of us who trailed the we
and followed them, but spoke less fluent

the avalanche bodies to the ruin
and then to the sea
not entirely yet now froze

and with gaps

between which we slipped, they closed over
soon after, the sea freeze came from the horizons towards
them as they stood to reach the coast zone

where last waves turning wet to froth, their reach reduced
amplitude low, and gave something to look at, the advance
and retreat of water, after which the freezing over of wet
and former undulation gave something else to look at too
until the cracks sealed that, and the sea and the flat
could not be distinguished from the other

the sand between long turned to glass, not sea glass
land glass no attrition, the dunes having nothing else to do
but unfurl their ovulation and fall to sea-level

the orb

endless horizons unchanging on approach, move and nothing shifts despite, the vista discloses no eruption into sight and seeing becomes equivalent to unseeing, with nothing to see in particular, all things to notice equal to zero, no things to notice, then, nor fixed point to determine a reason by
a decision, or a disavowal

a mere line division between this and that, this being nothing in particular, that being nothing to distinguish, a single line, full round and then some, no means to determine degrees of rotation, except other figures but figures move
nor way to judge the extent of one's advance or retreat
no progress nor regression, the beaten ground returns to glass before waymarks tell to where
neither view from the outside nor notion of an inside
no raising beyond the extent of their reach, no world above eight or nine feet, or the handspans their extended reach equated to so no roof either, a ceiling to determine perspective, to shelter, to present a second line between that
and there above.

With the flattening, their world became
the single line beyond reach
dividing nothing that had distinction before it was divided.

All flora forgotten entirely but the feel of it between teeth, rind, fibres
    the dune grass dead and fallen to ash amid the rest of it

no shore to stand at, the freeze had taken the upper layer of the sea to solid
    the zone gone between one thing and another at the surface of the flat, formerly between dry and wet, a place to reach from, to dwell along, to stand at, no wash to pass the feet nor shells to suck the living from.

Of those who still trod the flat we know nothing to
how long and how done
  and if the eat did finish them off before the drink

or the drink before the eat
or if in the wandering
or the standing, was their end despite the eat
    and the drink

each propelled by memory of consumption to eat, or do
like eat, though it did them under to do so

the eat be stone be dust be flat

each body become the flat, but determined

to face the eat, to pound the earth, and do the drink
persuaded by false recall of when the soil was raked
gathered, smelted, harvested, turned to product
destroyed, buried
and forgotten with the raking of new soil
called happiness and satisfaction and expenditure of want
called need   and this is not within our remit so, and do
not expect the earth, and give them a chance to deliver
and be realistic, please, and do not cross from one property
to the other without permission   or without taking
possession of the right to do unto others as they deserve
by the investiture of rank, due diligence, by the circulation
of resource, the permission of, to help themselves for their
share of what   the deliberate want of which
called accident of circumstance, that

take your foot off my mat, and fill this survey then, or just
leave a trail of seed, called fruit, of loins, of filth that will be
collected, and piled elsewhere until there is nowhere left to
shove it, still, build upwards
repaint surfaces, change the fixtures and
prevent the porches from becoming makeshift shelters

drive all things from sight that do displease and please the
right persons too, for the reason of the what, whichever
forget it

eat then eat

buy like eat

consume like eat, talk like eat

love like eat

the eat in all circumstances being

the grinding and the evacuation
of the eat from them
who ate for the purposes of the eat, none would say it is
not so.

Days before the flattening
were spent in ceaseless motion
some called it vigour, most called it work

and necessary, and had to be done

others called it a preparation for something else
unspecifiable, almost all failed to notice the expenditure of
energy that existence demanded of them, where sympathy

was, if it was

a recognition of this leakage in others, with
no option but the exhaustion of energies in moments, most
of which, not chosen but endured, not heroically, but
necessarily, and when recognised, retreated from
to the idol promise and the idol chamber.

Life was a matter of persistent exhaustion and eventual
collapse, not seen as such
but felt repeatedly and relegated to, then replaced
by
what, the what, the charm of sun on flesh and
autumn light, as the sloughed-off skin peeled into the
atmosphere and joined microscopic specks of plastic

shod cloth, soot, foot trod dirt, and the vast pollen excess
of the spring laid in the recesses between the furniture
and the wall, there was talk of a conspiracy, but human life
was not exhausted, as said

from serving as the head, and would
not be served better by those who abandoned it, as the
records did show to those who knew them those who
did abandon the head, or make something of their
madness died broken and then reborn, revived
poured over, written about, rose in their afterlife to
become figures of meaning, names, signifiers, put down, a
deposit, for the exhaustion of others, this exhaustion did
not appear, then, because humanity at last drained itself of
vitality in its effort to tell itself to itself as the reason of the
universe

the telling of itself to itself was just another reflex.

Human life was exhausted whether it served as the
head or not, reason of all, or naught before the vast
reaches of space

that life was servitude their servitude was
unavoidable

but human life was accustomed to the absurd
it could not sense its laughable destiny, enough reason to focus on
the excretory function.

Excreta were not so much examined, and picked over
those who give too much regard to the stool are
the sign of a world that has nothing to offer

each stool must be taken instead as the sign of death

the proximity of life to death, each excremental
a revelation, to nothing,

the conspirators did make a gift of it and deal death to one another, over dinner, offerings, naked and brought to vomit whilst on the street outside the carriages contained folk still the head of their world or so it was believed
as others walked alongside, feet in the muck, without a second set of clothes to retreat to, it being unknown if they looked, as they passed, for the reason of things, or not alongside those who served, so they thought, as the head of the world, organising perception, conveyed in

memoirs
science, and literary culture, that dirt refuses

and those in the rooms above as they dealt one another shit, refused also, or thought they refused, more openly but generated, even if, the act fabled or truly fabled, would lead to the death of the one served up the excreta

a closed circle of human digestion brings disease, sepsis
washed down, perhaps, with wine
but the grapes were dead before they were crushed
beetles crushed with them, the human jaw opening
it fell between one ramus and the other and never reached
the body, unlike the excreta that lined the mouth and
caused it to breathe death inward as much as outward.

What occurred, then, below in the city was likened
to an engine   indescribably productive but
productive of nothing
for the conspirators the destruction of the engine
was rendered impossible by its origins

in the energies of the sun

so the challenge was to destroy, artfully, completely, and
wage war on the materials accumulated, necessarily.

The production of ice, the entropic freeze
came to the consciousness of a later age
it did not figure in the imagination of those in

the rooms above, or the world they occupied, where excess
production is tied to the necessity of destruction, where
the precise means of destruction and the only choice
remaining to those who lived in such times is to destroy

how

by work, overwork, by reclining
by sleeping it out, by wandering
or mechanising, or asking why

by gorging oneself and launching satellites
and raking the sea, piling the earth

or by allowing all things to live unmolested

the lie of it that, but

the conspirators in the rooms above the street did present themselves with this decision and decided on their diet having only the engine in view   the prospect of unending production

of the ceaseless

overproduction of material

beyond the necessities of reproduction

and so.

With the freeze and the flattening the prospect altered

and the decision no longer appeared, the freeze was preceded by the flattening, that be said   with the flattening itself not a technological milestone but a disturbance in the fabric or so it was told, even words like these, of materials, of law of time, were soothing, when words were used, to all purposes, but mainly that, as they do under the ice, where speech is gone but phrases travel and carry their currencies and vaults and accidents to a diminishing consciousness.

There is light, but
the crustaceans avoid it
only the worms reach up from the seabed

admirers must
in the face of alterity, destroy despite themselves
they reek above where the air carries invading scent
a horrific bouquet   floral kitsch

the worms knew this as they reached for our behinds

travelled upward by the trunk of ice from the crust to the base

everything just proper, even done with irony, did stick in the maw and make retch

felt

false horns, and   stuffed cushions

dry rot spreading from the cellar nonetheless
to take the floor from its joists and drop the lot into the stink

china kitsch, spouts disgorging chamomile infused what

lithophane lamps

even plants native to subtropical zones produce daisies like every foul lawn in suburbia.

Lithops

fenestrated stones

lasted well into
the flattening
          and were

                    the model of the bomb, to cut the
earth with craters, submerge its people and fenestrate
them over

gorged, submerged
each eye almost fused to   the other

these would survive the flattening for the time that must

surely

come

if time did not halt at the reaches and
declare   the flat   our rift

in space
 and the end of an expanded
consciousness

the craters had to fill and become the flat, it will be so, but
new bombs   their release

no fall
the casement leaking its structures
the alloy in the craft will turn to vapour too, not crash
          to earth

like most that fly had eventually done, although the pilots
did crash to the flat, the rest become cloud, alloy levers
pulleys and tail fins be gas, plastics not so, these did
fenestrate in their descent, and   become corneas

slower as they fell, after

lingering

than the doomed pilots who
still heard the motors and propellers, these sublimated
irons emit

no sound except

the tone
of the reaches and crashed pilots, fenestrated

that was the last of the bomb

the prosthetic sea held attention for some moments

the scrapers alongside still rising to some
the extent of the internal walls not yet eroded, giving
the aspect of a

cliff

a backdrop for the chlorinated water
it presented a supplementary shore between the becoming
flat

of the earth that
  has no colour, and the sea becoming white with the
incoming freeze, the prosthetic sea between, azure

till it froze, and there was
in the reaches, nothing   between sky, and

surface.

Printed in Great Britain
by Amazon